dragonflies
codfish & frogs

By the same author
A THIN BODY OF WORK
SUNFLOWERS
LET IT BE A DANCE
HIS & HERS
THE VOICE OF THE HIVE
STARK NAKED
EVEN AS WE SPEAK
DESERTED ROOSTER

dragonflies codfish & frogs
formerly *SPEAKING POEMS*

by

Ric Masten

SUNFLOWER INK
Palo Colorado Canyon
Carmel, Calif. 93923

ACKNOWLEDGMENTS

A number of poems in this book first appeared in the booklets: *Who's Wavin',
Sunflowers,* and *Let It Be a Dance.* Also published by Sunflower Ink, Palo
Colorado Road, Carmel, CA 93923. Phone 408/625-0588.

Cover artwork Max-Karl Winkler
Graphics by Wilkins
Woodcuts by Ric Masten

DRAGONFLIES, CODFISH & FROGS produced by *Clack &
Nichols, A Partnership,* 403 North Texas, Odessa, Texas 79761

Originally published and printed in hardback and paperback
under the title SPEAKING POEMS by BEACON PRESS in
1977.

Third printing by SUNFLOWER INK 1979
    (paperback) 9 8 7 6 5

Copyright 1977 by Ric Masten

Library of Congress Catalogue Card No. 83-51803

ISBN 931104-14-9

All rights reserved. No part of this work may be reproduced or transmitted
in any form by an means, electronic or mechanical. Including photocopying
and or recording, or by any information storage or retrieval system, with-
out permission in writing from the publisher.

If the production and launching of this were a kite,
then heartfelt thanks must go to:

    Buz and Carol Johnson
    for the paper, sticks, and the Snappy Tom glue

    Uncle Frank and Aunt Ruth
    who have a place for flyers
    and a room with a view

    Chris Rawson
    who had much more than a hand in it

    David Fowler and Proctor Academy
    who helped me get it off the ground

    Dick Dunlop
    who believes the thing can fly

    Billie Barbara Masten
    who holds the string
    and
        keeps me on this side of the horizon

                *(and to Don Nichols
                and Cynthia Clack
                for the 2nd wind.)*

CONTENTS:

FOREWORD
by Roger Steffens   xiii

DRAGONFLIES   1

1. looking for patterns   4
2. a bell curve   5
3. ideas   6
4. inventing the wheel   7
5. cannibal   8
6. damn you gauguin
   and all other white whales   9
7. to a literary giant
   and other dare devils   10
8. published at last   11
9. three for anne sexton   12
10. another kind of noah   15
11. how to play the banjo   16
12. the price you pay
    for sunflowers   17
13. a moment of truth   19
14. a pulitzer prize winner   20
15. a sleeper   21
16. the writing on the wall   22
17. before mr. ford
    comes along mrs. james   23
18. an old hunter   24
19. on the mountain   25
20. where the poems come from   26

CODFISH   27

1. loneliness   30
2. the way to teach   32
3. grandparents/grandchildren   33
4. encounter   34

5. without kite and key   35
6. a place for conservatives   36
7. michelangelo   38
8. buel   39
9. the breakfast special   40
10. burning truth   41
11. house of grandfathers   42
12. a farm accident years ago   43
13. whales — off palo colorado   44
14. a loose end   45
15. a sneaking suspicion   46
16. the annual check up   47
17. the alternative   48
18. the second half   49
19. a kind of hope   50
20. on butterfly wings   51

& FROGS   53

1. mickey rooney/judy garland   56
2. a small quiet war   57
3. morning people vrs. night people   58
4. conversation   59
5. coming and going   60
6. robert and nancy   61
7. the hypothetical question   63
8. free at last   65
9. the time squeeze   66
10. waiting   67
11. white water   68
12. stop me if you've heard it   69
13. the bixby bridge incident   70
14. the quality of love   72
15. the chicago fire   73
16. afternoon tv   74
17. the counselor   75
18. the tower   76
19. a norman king   77
20. with a pierced ear   78

FINALE

    big sur country   81
    let it be a dance   83

THE SONGS

    the price you pay
      for sunflowers   87
    loneliness   90
    robert and nancy   92
    let it be a dance   94

AUTHOR'S NOTE

If this book should fall into your hands, my wish would be that you wouldn't read it but would find a friend to read it to you the first time through. To sit somewhere in the morning sun or by a window on a rainy afternoon, listening to the sound of this. What follows was meant to be said to you, not read by you and I believe the difference is the difference between feeling and thinking. I do not need your analytical mind stopping to measure the weight of these lines, I need your creative spirit flowing to help me free what the printer has locked up here.

Ric Masten

FOREWORD

Speaking Poems? What's this, some new subtext, some flashy buzzword, creating a heretofore unrecognized category? And who's speaking? Me? The Poet? Who's this book for, anyway?

Well, if you've completed even this first paragraph, then I can tell you, without fear of contradiction, that this book is for you. For Ric Masten comes as close to *speaking* for everyman as anyone alive in these Weighty Eighties. And no one works harder at milking the juice from the fruit of the language.

I must tell you a bit about my relationship with Ric, because in some ways we have been living similar lives since the mid-60s. My own one-man show is called "Poetry For People Who Hate Poetry", and I have performed it in 49 States: usually just before, or immediately after, Ric Masten was there. No matter how obscure a venue — Shelocta, Pa. or Fertile, Minnesota — Ric seems to have staked out his peculiar plot in the local territory. For ten years we dogged each others' footsteps. In a professor's basement in Ann Arbor, I'd be sent to bed with a pile of Masten's books, highly touted. It appears much the same thing happened with Ric as well. We were probably afraid to meet each other, the more the years went by. When you're doing something like Speaking Poems in a time of massive popular contempt for Poetry, you begin to feel like the lone voice in the wilderness. And you can get extremely uptight about any other folks out there "inventing the wheel" too.

Ultimately, though, a mutual friend in Riverside, Ca brought us together — with the most happy results. I was struck immediately at how the language transformed in Ric's mouth; the taut resonances of the nouns, the flexibility of his well-trained verbs. It seemed almost extemporaneous, the burst of fresh reasoning, spontaneously achieved. It was only when I lived on the

Mountain with Ric, that I saw the price he paid to achieve such effortlessness.

During the summer of 1978, my wife Mary and I were blessed beyond belief (considering we live near downtown LA in real life) by being able to live above Palo Calorado Canyon, in a glasswalled house facing the ocean, just beneath Ric's sprawling (handmade) home. Each morning we would meet at 9 for breakfast: Ric, as usual, having been awake from dawn, doing chores, picking up the mail. I was working on a couple of novels at this time — Ric on his yearly quota of new poems. Side-by-side we would sit on an overstuffed couch and compare the ten or fifteen pages of prose that I had churned out the previous day, with the few lines or stanzas that Ric had sweated out. Without question, the superior work was Ric's! How much more difficult to find that one, perfect and ineffable word that possesses within itself everything you are trying to pinpoint, all the peeks behind the mysterious folds and knots of the language. Ric would spend a whole day on a sentence. That's right, folks, from nine to five on the trail of a word. And that's his ultimate secret, the reason he sounds so informal (at his best).

Sophistication is *not* effortless — it just appears so. So my first piece of advice to you, dear reader, is not to be fooled by the "everydayness" of the speech in this book: it was definitely not "knocked off".

Speech. The central point. Because Ric and I (and our dwindling ilk) are Speakers. And as such, we want to speak nothing but the best ("and later for the garbage" as some old bluesman once said). There is an acid-like rush to wrapping your tongue around a great hunk of words, delicious chunk of onomatopoetic meat. The mouth tingles, the thoughtjuices come awash, the insights break through the dam of indifference. Ric makes you think. But, perhaps more important, Ric makes you laugh. Laughter heals like nothing else in the world. It is the secret of the universe, the sneaky surprise that removes the frown of "serious thinking" that's caused so much of our world's anxieties. And the gift that Ric has given us in these pages, and others, is the chance to shape in our own mouths the sudden leaps from behind the doors of perception. READ THIS BOOK OUT LOUD! Read it to your lover, your teacher, your brother whom you haven't spoken to in five years. Read it for the joy that you will find on their faces; color it with the nuances of your own perceptial pallette.

    This book, in fact, is a readers theater play, and has been performed as such on many campuses in America. One recent production has the Dragonfly section divided among four men and five women and an additional "narrator" who represents Ric himself. This opening group of poems is set in a madhouse. The Ric figure explains what a speaking poem is, dressing in institutional white as he talks. Eventually the curtains open and he joins the other ten. The Codfish section is an airport, with Ric's interpreter indicated by a distinguishing characteristic, like a pair of glasses. The Frog section is in an Esalen-like group therapy session, with all the actors wearing the trademark glasses. Finally, when the curtains close, all come forward, removing their glasses. "I am you, as you are me, and we are all together" as another legend-inspiring performer once noted.

    If you've never had the experience of a lifetime, and heard Ric perform his work in person, or played records of his shows, then I advise this. Slip into something, and somewhere, comfortable. Flip the book at random and speak aloud the first thing you come to. Like reading the Bible and the I Ching, you'll really just be talking to yourself.

Roger Steffens
Los Angeles, Jan. 1981

dragonflies

Rather than the usual numbers, I have chosen three creatures to head up the sections of this book. Three living things that symbolize, at least for me, the themes I will be touching on.

Here in this first group of poems, to express the pain and joy of the creative act, I choose the Dragonfly. An insect that spends its life both beneath and above the surface of things. At the bottom, subterranean and grotesque at times, but like the poet and artist splitting his own skin to emerge, rising up winged and iridescent.

i wish i could remember
what i knew when i was five
i think i had the answer then
having just recently arrived

i recall
that i could change into a dragonfly
and when you know how to do this
you know everything

no wonder i cried
when they sent me off
on that first day of school

1. LOOKING FOR PATTERNS

i collect small
typewritten words
and fly them
    looking for patterns

sometimes they rise from me
in clouds
like birds off a field
to circle and then wheel away
for no apparent reason
    and i
lie empty as a pasture
left behind
defined only by these dark fences
of mine

    western civilization
    waiting for the punch line

missing the point

2. A BELL CURVE

if your carpenter
didn't know what batterboards were
you are probably living in a lopsided house
the carpenter's apprentice
will carry and stack a lot of lumber
learning his trade

and when it comes to brain-surgeons
i believe in grades
bell curves and all that
i want to see him flunked out
long before he gets into my head
asking a nurse
what all the funny looking wrinkled stuff is
and god help the electrical engineer
who gets his wires crossed

but how do you grade a poem?

i mean wouldn't it be a little bit
like trying to grade a dream

     ah — student
     your dream started off well enough
     but fell all apart in the middle
     too much sex for sex sake
     and the ending was quite frankly trite
     at best this is a C- dream

parents — faculty — students — friends
what we have here is the finest trade school
in the history of the world
     period
so let's hear it for today's tool and die makers
and leave the dreamers be

3. IDEAS

they strike when least expected
and with each bite a rush of excitement
has me dropping everything
grabbing at the line
to find most often nothing
    there at all
except the feeling of a dream
i know i had but can't recall

i do my fishing on the other side
and if i'm lucky
clean them over here
    like this one
i got yesterday in a restaurant
on a paper napkin that never touched my mouth

it's not much to brag about
    being small
and rather insignificant
but may i say
poet to poet
you should have seen the ones that got away

4. INVENTING THE WHEEL

i don't often read other poets
and i'll tell you why

when i finally get around
to sitting down in the middle of the road
to invent the wheel
having spent days
gathering my materials around me
and having just figured out where to drill
the first hole
it's enough to make you break down and cry
to look up and see
some brilliant young S.O.B.
on a bicycle
              go pedaling by

5. CANNIBAL
*(This for all poets
I have carefully avoided.)*

    i see by the posters
you gave a reading at the forum last night
i didn't forget
i just didn't attend

had the meal tasted as good
as i suspected it would
foolishly
i'd feel diminished
if undigestible
the evening wasted
either way i spared myself what would have been
a miserable ordeal

if you have anything to do with poetry
i think you'll know and understand
how difficult it is
to go and watch someone else serve up
the eucharist
to sit behind a hand and analyze the footwork
holding back petrified
that you'll get out of control
        and eat it up
        and enjoy it

a reformed cannibal
can't be too careful
so i keep myself away from any kind
of plump juicy missionary
and dine alone on my own
        cold potatoes

6. DAMN YOU GAUGUIN
   AND ALL OTHER WHITE WHALES

for someone caught in the paper claw
of a corporate world
the watercolor
hanging in his office
was good enough to be terribly distracting
he had talent alright
enough to keep one small part of his mind
    waving free
like ahab's arm
beckoning from that elusive dream

> but how do you ask an orthodontist
> to take the bands off the kid's teeth
> i mean
> do you go to him and say
> remove the braces dr. bently
> i'm running off to the islands
> to be an artist
> i can't afford them anymore
> or do you get a pair of pliers
> and do it yourself

the young and romantic
might find this hard to believe
but you simply cannot get to tahiti from here

7. TO A LITERARY GIANT
AND OTHER DARE DEVILS

if i acted crazy — forgive me
but i'm a daredevil too
and when i arrived at the jump site
and saw the monstrous crowd pressing around you
i was afraid you might not see my bike

but you gave me a tired smile
and waved from the foot of the ramp
a marvelous feat considering all the distractions

out on the edge a promise
is a dangerous contraption
having little to do with bravery

>   if you can't say No
>   your Yes means nothing

and you are much too valuable
to waste on the snake river

8. PUBLISHED AT LAST

    on the river there has been a separation
    and we don't know where he is
    but she
    slender as a water weed slipped past
    bleeding darkly from the broken place

        appearing
    briefly in the rapids
    swept along waving bravely
    throwing kisses
    as only she could do

        we tried to reach her
        but the current was too strong

    that was yesterday
    her eyes like great
    dark stones still weight
        me down
            beneath the surface
    of her much deserved success

9. THREE FOR ANNE SEXTON

1.

your poetry
    is not a pleasant thing
    all sunshine and butterflies
    passing into oblivion
    uneventful
    as a lazy summer afternoon

not at all
    it comes down on me
    the work of a distressed angry bee
    and where it hits me
    does not feel good

your stinger
    stinging me and stinging me
    till my whole being
    swells up with ideas
    painful enough to bring me wide awake

and sometimes
i hate you for it

2.

anne
i suffer the fate of a fan

(June, 1974)

      i read your poems today
      rode them like horses
      magnificent beasts
      and i was impressed with the way
      you've harnessed your pain
          with the way
      you've kept yourself sane
      riding those
             wild
                  twisting
                        dreams
                              down
to a standstill
down to a fanfare
      admiring the way you could trot them around
      under perfect control
      no wonder they gave you
          the prize
      but the photograph on the dust cover
      the cow puncher face
      the big floppy hat
      i could have done without that
      and the terrible hurt in your eyes

(October of the same year)

      and now they tell me
      you've gone down under the hooves
          with sylvia
      anne
      was there ever a dream
          couldn't be rode
          or a dreamer
              couldn't be throwed

3.

      poets
      are a skittish breed of cat
      crouching in the doorway
      we make our presence known
careful
      where we put our feet
we must be

      for there is only one room in the house
      and in it two voices
one that shouts
out cat out

the other calling
come kitty
pretty kitty

      there was this over-sensitive siamese
      and she could only hear the anti-voice
      the dark one

but jesus
she described it well
filling books with the pitch
      timber and tone
      the awful sound
that hounded her childhood
ruined her youth
and finally chased her off
to curl up and die alone
out in the garage

      poor pitiful thing
      shouted down
      by a half truth

10. ANOTHER KIND OF NOAH

and yet when my friend marvin
the mad poet comes out of the zoo
every six months
      one shoe on
      one shoe off
i'm always glad to see he isn't cured
that he still limps in his mind
      old nutty marv
because you know i really don't want
to run the instant replay
of yesterday's baseball game
i need his insane rhymes
like straws to clutch at
not the box score — i watch him

      paul gauguin
watching through his own window pain
his crazy friend
      vincent
winding his head up in gauze
knowing the hurt to be the very ground
in which art grows
and far better for him at least
than filling galleries with slick paintings
of wet city streets — colors reflecting
or of little kids with big sad eyes
at fifty bucks a throw

and though it seems unfair of me
i need him there — at sea
      adrift
      tending his mad menagerie
      another kind of noah

i need him there — dropping me a line
each time i fall
into that awful
      blue period of mine

11. HOW TO PLAY THE BANJO

no
even if i could have
    i would not have
spared van gogh the pain of cutting
    his ear off
and robbed myself of those sunflowers
sorry about that vincent
sorry about that
    myself
and yet
for you who say be totally sensitive
know that i once knew a ditch digger
who bled to death in his own trench
because he could not grow a callus
    couldn't play banjo either
without cutting himself to ribbons
    on the wires

i need my thick skin for protection
otherwise i couldn't say anything
    of consequence
without breaking down completely
right here in front of you
    and you wouldn't want that now
    would you

total sensitivity
    well
it's sort of like an orgasm
you can only stand just so much of it
before you go right out of your gourd

12. THE PRICE YOU PAY FOR SUNFLOWERS
(Song poem, music on pages 87, 88, 89)

you come out of that place again
i gaze into your face again
try to read your eyes again
today
you walked right in and sat awhile
stroked the striped cat awhile
just as tho you'd never been away

and when i asked you how you'd been
you looked up from the cat and then
you sang a song so tender and so strange
closed your eyes and let it come
and when you finally get it sung
you answered
oh — i'm just about the same

> sunflowers
> time and time again
> i need to spend an hour
> with my sunflower friend
> sunflowers
> light the way
> put a touch of color
> in the long dark day

i offered you a cup of tea
the way that you looked up at me
i knew you hadn't heard a word
i said
your mind so full of crows in flight
and pinwheel spinning starry nights
and no time in the dream to rest your head

but time is for the ticking clock
and you're between the tick and tock
bleeding from the passion in your brain
so put another bandage on

and sing us all another song
and fill us
with the beauty and the pain

       of sunflowers
       time and time again
       i need to spend an hour
       with my sunflower friends
       sunflowers
       light the way
       put a touch of color
       in the long dark day

the afternoon is dying fast
your songs are bits of flying glass
the colored edges cut into
my eyes
and looking through the salty mist
i saw that you knew how to risk
and father said — all else is a lie

and when you couldn't take no more
you went out through an open door
looking for your blinding field of hay
you left us rich but feeling sad
'cause you were sane and we were mad
but i guess
that's the price you pay

       for sunflowers

13. A MOMENT OF TRUTH

in some other life
i must have been a bull fighter
a little spanish rooster
    hot stuff
    in my suit of lights
but not so hot on sleepless nights
my mind out there in the pens
where the bulls wait like mountains
    dark premonitions
    milling around
    restless
all my brave tomorrows

    hey amigo
    tell me
    is this where
    you really want to be

no not at all

except
in the afternoon
when there is no time to think
and hats are flying thick as crows

except
when i consider doing something
less dangerous for my sunflowers

except
when i parade through the kitchen
with a bleeding ear like this — held high

the fruit of the day
the prize
    and perhaps from you
    a small
    ole

14. PULITZER PRIZE WINNER

    of louis simpson i knew nothing
    except that he had won the pulitzer prize
    for poetry

    so when i saw that he also
    was visiting the university of michigan
    i went to hear him read
        to sit beforehand watching
    while other interested students and faculty
    trickled in chattering lightly nonchalant

    amusing myself by trying to pick
        our prize winner
    out of the crowd up front
    and while doing this realized
    that everyone in the room
    was the picture of a poet
        young and flowing
        old and fussy

    finally
    arriving down the aisle
    simpson was there
    looking like a certified public accountant

        by the clock
        he took exactly
        one hour of my time

    afterward
    crunching along
    through a crisp ann arbor afternoon
    i considered
    getting a haircut

15. A SLEEPER

to be a poet reading
is chancy work at best
tough enough to face rejection
but worse
far worse this:

you fell asleep
even as i read you closed your eyes
and dropped your head upon your chest
and to this day i marvel
that you kept your seat
        nodding
          east and west

and although i find it sad
i guess it's only human
that looking back upon a sea
of open faces
i can best recall the one that slept
and wonder
were you overtired
        or simply bored
with all that i expressed

only now writing this
years later
have i thought to ask about the dream
you might have had that day
and all
        i may have missed

16. THE WRITING ON THE WALL

if we show them at all most of us
who write our secrets down and call it poetry
prefer to slip it under the door and run
and if we must be present at the reading
disguise ourselves
      in soto voce and pale monotone

but here was one who could take us
into his personal life and show us around
as if it were a house for sale
exposing everything the way it was
and never once it seemed rushing ahead
to straighten up a room or kick the dirty linen
      underneath a bed

i got my questions ready
how could he do it — and why
it was such private property
and we were total strangers
just in off the street — looking
not necessarily there to buy
but then toward the end of the tour
i realized there was nothing in this place
i hadn't seen before
and when i told him this at the door
he took me by the hand and thanked me
      for helping him feel so at home

outside as we were leaving
i saw where some street philosopher
had taken paint
and sprayed a classic on the wall

      there are no strangers here — it read
      i know myself
      therefore
            i know you all

17. BEFORE MR. FORD
    COMES ALONG MRS. JAMES

    let me say
    i have done this long enough to know
        i don't write my poems
        we do
    and so i live much like
    that indistinct little man in western movies
    the one in shirt-sleeve and vest
    who seems to exist only at the window
    of the telegraph office
        never shot
        never kissed
    his reason for being
    simply a gimmick to further the plot

        like him
    i sit at the end of my pen
        hunched over
    sending and receiving
    taking the messages down
    reading them back to you

        and this just came over the wire

GOOD NEWS STOP EVERY HUMAN RELATIONSHIP
THAT HAS EVER BEEN OR WILL EVER BE ENDS STOP
GOOD NEWS ONLY IF WE USE THE INFORMATION
AND TELL THE PEOPLE WE LOVE THAT WE LOVE
THEM AND DO IT TODAY STOP TOMORROW IS
ONLY A FIGMENT OF OUR IMAGINATION STOP

        I LOVE YOU

        JESSE

18. AN OLD HUNTER
(for Robinson Jeffers)

i found him reflecting
in his stone tower
       alone
his profile against the window
poet
why so silent in these your latter days
have you nothing more to say?

i was coming on strong — fat
with young ideas
beating the bushes
shooting at everything in sight
he turned his face to mine

      when you have said
      what it is you have to say
      and played all the obvious variations
      you will learn to sit quietly
      in the afternoon
      and listen to the thicket

and thus i left him
just off the trail
an old hunter
waiting for the game
to come to him

      one shell
      left
      in the chamber

19. ON THE MOUNTAIN

somewhere about a third of the way up
he came striding down the trail
and caught me unaware
a poet
staff in hand — naked — thin as a whip
wild gray hair framing the sunstained face
his bright eyes blue holes
                the sky showing through

when he saw me resting there
he laughed out loud
    friend, he said
      i have been to the summit
             and found nothing there
              absolutely nothing
then laughing again
he went on down around the bend
           and left me

with my brand new dayglow knapsack
ten dollar compass — waterproof boots
remembering how i'd sharpened my knife
till it shaved the hair
on the back of my wrist
preparing myself for almost anything but this

still i was young then
and it wasn't until i too
had run out of places to climb
           that i began to wonder
where he was going and what he was after
             laughing that way
and so turning around
             i followed on down behind

and if i took you by surprise
this morning coming down the path
believe me i was only laughing at my self
           sitting there

20. WHERE THE POEMS COME FROM
(To an idea of Robert Blys)

it is dark
on the underside of morning
for me it is
and anxiety waits here
a cold blooded reptile
coiled into a sluggish knot
a hunger that keeps the birds away
whispering
        fear
        fear
        fear

          i retreat
to exorcise with barbara walters
who became jane pauley
brewing coffee
and while doing this
watch the field from the window
sometimes a three legged fox appears
not every day but when she does
she kills and eats the lizard

and what i was feeling turns around
becoming what it always was

        a tool to use
        a wand to wave

till afternoon and evening vanish
and i can see the voice of a lark
an illusion — true
but one that sheds light on everything
and makes it look so easy

at least till
night descends the capstone under which it all
    begins   again

codfish

When they are landed, codfish must find the space we call reality a hard place to be.

In this section I will verbalize awhile on the real world, or at least the one I think I see. Racially, religiously, conservatively speaking, I view the human dilemma as terribly funny at times. I mean it can be really laughable, unless of course there is something fishy about your sense of humor.

a squirming trophy
delivered rudely
with a slap and a shout
to agonize on the paradox

        one eye down
        on the dark souring wharf
        the other up
        in a towering sky

born
beginning to die
    i am
like a codfish
flopping about
at the edge of all this
    in and out
        of my element

1. LONELINESS
(Song poem, music on pages 90, 91)

standing by a highway
waiting for a ride
a bitter wind is blowing
keeps you cold inside
a line of cars is passing
no one seems to care
you look down at your body
to be sure you are there

sitting in a hotel
staring at the walls
with cracks across the ceiling
and silence in the halls
you open up the window
and turn the TV on
then you go down to the lobby
but everybody's gone

    and this is loneliness
the kind that i have known
if you've had times like this
    my friend
    you're not alone

so you leave the empty city
and go down to the shore
you're aching to discover
what you're looking for
the beaches are deserted
in the morning time
a solitary figure
you walk the water line

come upon a tidepool
and stand there peering in
and when you touch the water
the circles do begin

they lead to where a seabird
lies crumpled on the sand
so you take a single pebble
and hold it in your hand

    and this is loneliness
another kind i've known
if you've had times like this
    my friend
    you're not alone

you come back up the beaches
at the end of day
and see how all your footprints
have been washed away
no
nothing is forever
we are born to die
so may i say i love you
before i say goodbye

    i must say i love you
    before i say goodbye

2. THE WAY TO TEACH
*(It isn't so much having a question
to ask, rather the ability to create one)*

and so
he let them have their games
until the tide was fully out
    and when it was
he came upon the rocky beach
a may-pole of a man
among the shouting children
and bending down beside a magic pool
    peering in
he waited
till a ring of faces gathered
at the edge of this attention
then slowly reaching through the mirror
gave a sea anemone
    a punch
who did what sea anemones will do
quickly folding in
on what should have been a lunch

    WOW!

he said — eyes popping
then abruptly rising
but keeping in mind the length of his legs
moved on up the beach
    the children scrambling behind
    with questions

3. GRANDPARENTS/GRANDCHILDREN

trying hard to understand human nature
i
having pacifist leanings
find my son learning karate
breaking bricks with his bare hands
so that he could kill a man
in two seconds
he says smiling
as i go up the wall

and i
being the son of militant ex-catholic
atheist parents
get myself ordained a minister
much to the disgrace of my old mother
whose reedy voice calls me on the phone

>ricky! — she squeaks

as always speaking
like a punch and judy show
and i as always looking
for the alligator to jump up
and hit her with a stick

>ricky! — she squawks

>you're not gonna let them
>put Reverend in front of your name
>in the phone book are you?

now
i suppose all this explains
why the grandparents and the grandchildren
usually get along so well

they have a common enemy

4. ENCOUNTER

it was just that i was
very touchy that day
and really that's
all i can say
to explain why
while walking through
the sears & roebuck department store
i happened to get into
this fist fight with a mannequin

5. WITHOUT KITE AND KEY

i can understand the stove
    the bifocal
    and some of the other stuff
but benny
without the kite and the key
what in hell is electricity
and please spare me
    the zero/infinity
    form of energy routine
seeming to this untutored mind
a kind of doctrinal line
demanding a greater leap of faith
than a catholic or a baptist makes

it strikes me . . . (a little electrical
                    engineering humor there)

that you
who believe in electricity
should wear a habit and shave your head
to go with the mystical smile that you smile
while seeing the light
pretending you know what goes on

you may be pious enough
to actually own a phillips screwdriver
one of the chosen few
but where is the juice
when the generator shuts down

    like the spirit and soul
    of the dear departed
    where has it gone?

6. A PLACE FOR CONSERVATIVES

    i must admit it bothers me more
    than just a little bit
    to see an airline pilot with dandruff
    sitting around
    slightly wrinkled
    chewing gum
    looking like any one of us
        i mean
    when you see the crew
    go passing through the gate
    don't you want the captain
        to be a tight-lipped man
        with close cropped hair
        eyes like steel doors slammed shut
        crisp white shirt
        slacks creased so sharply
        if you weren't careful
        you could get a nasty cut there

    why i'd turn in my boarding pass
    just like that
    if some freaky long-haired cat
    came bopping by
    with an earring on one side
    saying

        hey baby
        i'm gonna take us for a ride

    believe me i'm finally convinced
    there really is a place for conservatives
    or would you go to a neurosurgeon
    who bit his fingernails—
    seen knocking his drink over all the time
        i mean
    would you really want to do business
    with either one of these guys
    the morning after

he fought all night with his wife

        not on your life
        not me at least
        if i'm getting on that plane
        going under that knife

what we need here
are hard minded
cold blooded
machine-like people
in a culture as techno-
logically advanced as ours has become
        we cannot all afford to be
            human

7. MICHELANGELO

    high in the scaffolding on his back
    michelangelo bites his lip — sighs
    and then begins to paint the hand of god
        down

        below
    sweeping the chapel floor
    a little serf leans his broom against the wall
    squints up
    and with an arm full of trash
    stumbles out through a graceful arch
    mumbling to himself

        damn faggots

8. BUEL

i've seen the eyes lookin'
at my beard in the mississippi airport
    i've seen prejudice — hell
i've hid in the men's room — two hours
waiting for my plane — just showin' my feet
    i've seen prejudice — but you're right
i can shave it off
i'll never see those eyes lookin' out from inside
    black skin

buel
have you ever seen a honky and felt anythin'
but anger — maybe envy?
have you ever looked at your black brother
and felt anythin' but pride — maybe shame?
how about guilt
    you ever felt that lookin' at me — i do
    lookin' at you
not because my people did your people over
my people also worked kids to death in the
work house
fed christians to lions — burned witches too
but that was my people — not me
and i ain't gonna hang in my family tree

i'm only guilty of being unable to ignore the
    color of your skin
like i was taught i was supposed to do
when i was a kid and there ain't any way
you could know about this
    being black
    or for me to tell you being
white

but buel
i been lonely
can you understand that?

9. THE BREAKFAST SPECIAL

        a toasted english muffin
        with whipped creamy butter
        and a steaming mug
        of mountain grown coffee
it all sounds so good on the menu
    fresh ranch eggs
conjuring up pictures of
mother, father and i on an outing
flying through a summer countryside
in an open tin lizzy
mother holding her floppy hat in the wind
laughing. . . . banjo music playing
and chickens everywhere!   scattering
scurrying back to a barn
full of sunshine cracks and aromatic shadows
where clucking hens nest in secret places
laying eggs for children to find
put into baskets and bring us for breakfast
        yes i'll have some of that this morning.

pretending i've not
been to the concentration camp
and seen the eyes staring through the wire
and seen the miles and miles
of shopping basket cells
with barely room enough to move or sleep
forgetting how they helplessly stand for days
eating off tin trays
drinking from galvanized tanks
watching their lifes work roll away like teeth

taken out of the circle of things
    crispy bacon strips
    and country cured ham
have nothing to do with the slaughter.

    we eat words   and no one says grace
                                  and no one gives thanks

10. BURNING TRUTH

the mail comes
and i lose another friend today
to sweet jesus

head bowed
i read the news written in your own hand
somehow antiseptic now
on the cleanest piece of paper
i have ever seen

> praise be to god
> praise god
> over and over and over

you gave the answers
from beginning to end
with no space left
for walking mountain roads again
two men
talking in the twilight
playing with the questions

> god knows
i need a crutch at times
to get this gimpy soul of mine around
but not a burning truth that we must
> kill each other over

11. HOUSE OF GRANDFATHERS

in the house of grandfathers
the dusty old flowers sit around
fishing for smiles
sometimes they read stories to themselves
from torn yellow pages
and it is amusing for awhile
but they know why i come

    it looks like hard work old man
    and no one to lend a hand
    except well meaning girls coming
    like hornets with their stingers
    getting in your way with cylinders — tubes
    and see-through tents

it seems to me if you were home
you'd be done with your labor
and resting already

    i kept the watch awhile but couldn't stay

good-by old man — old dandelion
i wish i were the wind

12. A FARM ACCIDENT YEARS AGO

the horses shied and then wild-eyed
bolted from the field
racing back toward the barn
traces flying
the mower still attached
and running close behind
your father
shouting an alarm
as that ugly snapping arm
reached out
taking everything off at the ankle
weeds and corn and hollyhock
and then in slow motion
sweeping through the stems
of two small boys frozen in surprise

      and sometime later
in a photograph we find
those grinning little peg legged petes
proud as punch
posing
      though the color and shape
      are exactly right
      an artificial limb
      is what it is
      and can be put on and taken off

      but the story that comes with it

walks
and walks and walks

13. WHALES — OFF PALO COLORADO

today i saw the whales
moving south along the coast
and had to stop the car and get out
and stand there just watching

one of them came in close to shore
and i thought to myself then
that the whole journey would be worth it
just to see the magic of this atlantis — rising
blowing and steaming from the sea — an island
of life
      today i saw the whales and i was healed

i can tell you now of the dancers — the three girls
and the dark wet highway — and the car
that came hurtling into their young lives
and how the rain fell for five days as we followed
slowly behind black limousines — three times
slowly with our lights on

but the sun returned this morning
and the rain has washed the air clean
and brought the ventana mountains in so close
they cut my eyes
      sometimes it hurts to see things clearly

for those girls the dance had just begun
but they went out dancing
trailing veils behind them and somehow
this simple act tells me that they too paused
somewhere along the way and saw
      the whales moving south along the coast
      on a day like today

i hope you will forgive me
for trying to put order and sense to it all
but if i don't can you tell me
      who in hell will?

14. A LOOSE END

       it's true i've put off
dealing
       with one aspect of my father's life
       a loose end so to speak
       perhaps because he died when i was so young
       and i remember him not so much as a person
       but more of a presence
          a feeling

       so it's not him that i must
finally
       get around to, rather the end of him
       he was forty-nine when he passed away
       i was twelve—and he seemed older than god then
       but now with me at forty-six i can see
          he was in his prime and his
          untimely

       death is what really has me
bothered
       the shadow of this event just ahead
       the date crossing my path—an open fracture
       in the shape of a question mark
       i ask myself
       could i ever be older than
          my father?

       and a kind of panic
fills me
       to break through the barrier
       and find myself alone on the other side
       without him
       i think i'd rather die first
       and in the next three years if i'm not careful
       this could be the loaded gun that just might
          kill me

15. A SNEAKING SUSPICION

i have given my pets the power
and let my little dog amazing grace
get such a grip on me
that more than once i've folded maps
and called off an extended trip
it becoming more than i can bear
to watch her napping in the sun so unaware
trusting to the moment
oblivious to the desire
     of man and flea

the side of me that lags behind
and drags its feet
gets hold of my imagination
till i have myself confined
in the wire world of the kennel
waiting in canine limbo
brave and stoic
with pricked ears listening
keeping watch on the door
expecting each moment to be the moment
     the master reappears

and i do this to myself
till i must cancel travel plans
deciding not to go
unable to stand the thought
of missing myself so

that
and the sneaking suspicion
that once on the road
i'll forget her as quickly as i
will be replaced by something
     alive and moving in the brush

16. THE ANNUAL CHECK UP

every now and then i discover this
    strange lump
in my abdomen which i finger
when no one is looking to see if
    the soreness
is still there and it always is
and so in fear and trembling i go
to see my doctor and hear
    the bad news
and this kindly old bird hops around me
like a crow with a piece of tin foil
poking and peering
until stroking his chin he declares
that i am in A-1 condition and if i'd stop
handling my pancreas it wouldn't be
    so sore

and yet always in the end
i leave his office with the certain knowledge
that i will be
    dead
in six months the good doctor keeping my
    awful infirmities
from me so that i can enjoy what little time
i have left and bravely with this information
hidden under my coat i return home
to be with my family and together
we climb the hill in back of the house
to sit a spell
and really watch a cloud move

i guess you'd say
i was a bit of a hypochondriac and that's OK
it keeps me close to things
and on this ward we are all
    terminal
anyway

17. THE ALTERNATIVE

imagine
that it wasn't me
you came here to see today
rather the statesman
        comic
        entertainer
        philosopher
        theologian
that you admire the most

the he or she
who has driven a line of words
into your life   -
    an idea
like the pin into a hinge
and you moved on it

arriving early to assure yourself
of a good seat
you would find tacked to the door
    the small print
stating that it was true
your idol was here
but if you came inside
you would have to remain till the end
of the program
which would last for eternity

        every one of you
        would have turned away
        at the door i believe
        so don't tell me
        you want to live forever

death
will lose its sting
only after
you consider the alternative

18. THE SECOND HALF

i turned forty a while ago
and came dribbling out of the locker room
ready to start the second half
glancing up at the scoreboard
i saw that we were behind
    7 to 84
and it came to me then
    we ain't gonna win
and considering the score
i'm beginning to be damn glad
this particular game ain't gonna go on
    forever

but don't take this to mean i'm ready
for the showers
take it to mean i'm probably gonna play
one hellava second half

i told this to some kids in the court
next to mine and they laughed
but i don't think they understood
    how could they
playing in the first quarter only one point
    behind

deep into autumn
the third period
i have discovered
that winning the game
is not what is important

what is important though
is
that i look good
while losing

19. A KIND OF HOPE

    i guess you'd call him a revolutionary
    but he laughed real laughter
    and when he was quiet his eyes were sad
    so i hung around and listened to him talk

    he said
        we have broken the ocean beyond repair
        the crabs are leaving
        we will soon follow

    he said
        we live in an insane asylum
        where the sensitive must go insane
        that is to say go sane
        and then must kill the pain
        with pill and needle

    he said
        the next time the conquering heroes arrive
        the future is gone in a nuclear flash

    he said
        and there is no time left for the corn
        to grow

    but the fact that he bothered to get out of bed
    this morning and say it gives me
        a kind of hope

20. ON BUTTERFLY WINGS

you know for the life of me
i can't recall what happened
last good friday
christmas i can
because mother got smashed
and the baby seeing his image distorted
on the surface of a thousand ornaments
    cried all day
and on easter it rained
so that the candy hidden
in the grass got sticky
and we had to wash the ants off
before we let the kids out but somehow i missed
    good friday

looking the other way i guess
like i do
when i pass someone walking the roadside with an
    empty gas can
muttering under my breath
about the high cost
    of funerals
and how the undertakers are bleeding us dry
    like vampires
not stopping to realize
we can't pay those guys enough to handle
what scares us half to
    death

i mean
if aunt maude bites the bag in my kitchen
you're gonna find me outside in the yard waiting
    for some weird cat
to roll up in a long black vehicle
and clean up the mess — cart the problem away
    smiling all the while

oh
i'll stop by the parlor saturday afternoon

check the flowers out
and have a quick look in the box
but then i never was able
to accept a gift graciously
and it's my loss and no doubt the reason
i sit in my own small house drinking coffee
    feeling homesick most of the time

an old guru once told me
that the only thing
we really have to do in this life
    is die
and i think i shall repeat this statement
over and over
a hundred times each night before i
    go to sleep
perhaps if i could bring myself to believe it
i mean really believe it
and remember what happens
    on good friday
i just might come out and find myself
some sunny easter morning
    on butterfly wings
    rising

& frogs

Without all the croaking who would know there was anyone else in the pond, and so a few words about interpersonal communication and the importance of same. And as you wade through here on your way to the "finale" keep in mind that there is a lot more going on between the princess and the frog than mere kisses.

once upon a time
a warty frog
had a princess come along
and kiss it
    nothing happened

but when another frog
hopped up
    something did

and for those of you
wondering what to do
while waiting
for your prince to come
i say
    enjoy the frog

1. MICKEY ROONEY / JUDY GARLAND

with a kind of early mickey rooney
judy garland innocence we go before the church
and state exchanging unspoken trust
for legal documents the soul intent of which
is meant to cover and protect
all moon struck lovers from themselves
when later in the course of human events
comes the expected divorce and property settlement

the magic and excitement traded off
for false security — signed — sealed
and written down — the guarantee
that neither he nor she will ever screw around

and didn't we go down beneath the weight
of that iron bouquet
dead
preserved in the state of wed-LOCK
and is it any wonder that pickled in this
atmosphere
the act of love becomes a habit
like eating in a chinese restaurant
only because it's close and handy
sitting down together with the empty sound
of clicking silverware and nothing left between
but pork chow mein and strained silence
the bill always coming with fortune cookie wisdom
like
    he who catches bus
    will never have to chase it

and other sad commentaries
written by some poor sap and his wife
trapped forever in a cookie factory
on the outskirts of every city and town
in america

2. A SMALL QUIET WAR

and she's at it again — my wife
under the house
digging

i can hear her down there
with my old rusty tools
picking
and shovelling away
hollowing out a place
for her imagination
to run wild in

she's been at it
off and on
for two years now
running back and forth
with one shovel full of dirt
at a time
throwing it into the yard
doing it the hard way
and i must admit i'm always surprised
and a bit annoyed
when i see the size of the pile
she is making
but it's her project
and she says
i'm not and don't have to be
involved

still and all
it has now become impossible
for me
to lie here comfortably
listening to the ball game

3. MORNING PEOPLE vrs. NIGHT PEOPLE

    according to morning people
night people are necrophiliacs
       lying dead to the world
       coming to life only when the light fails
       hinged at the waist
       lifting slowly like coffin lids
       they rise pale as the moon
       to go about their dark murky business
       their mad jerky dance
       till the crack of dawn
       has them cowering back behind a hand
       shrinking from the very thought
       of a hearty breakfast
       creeping away they sleep with salamanders
while morning people shower
brush their teeth and rush to meet the day

to night people however
morning people seem to be
       perverted jogging machines
       getting off on self punishment
       kinky types — sweaty — breathing hard
       in love with their own shoes
       flagelators
       whipping themselves along
       with an unsmiling determination
       that smacks of hitlers youth
       there is something rather nazi
       about a flat belly
       and something terribly immoral about people
       who go to bed with john chanselor

either way
it's really not a question of wrong or right
it's just that some demons
won't let you sleep in the morning
and some demons keep you awake in the night

4. CONVERSATION

i have just wandered back
into our conversation
and find that you are still rattling on
about something or other
i think i must have been gone at least
twenty minutes
and you never missed me

now this might say something
about my acting ability
or it might say something about
your sensitivity

one thing troubles me though
when it is my turn to rattle on for twenty
minutes which i have been known to do
have you been missing too?

5. COMING AND GOING

    i have noticed
    that men
    somewhere around forty
    tend to come in from the field
    with a sigh
    and removing their coat in the hall
    call into the kitchen
                    you were right
                    grace
                    it ain't out there
                    just like you've always said
    and she
    with the children gone at last
    breathless
    puts her hat on her head

                    the hell it ain't

    coming and going
    they pass
    in the doorway

6. ROBERT AND NANCY
(Song poem, music on page 92, 93)

    robert
    buried in the tribune with his coffee
    reading all about the day before
    nancy
    just across the table with her teacup
    studies what the tea leaves hold in store
        and the now
        the moment slips away
        gone with its joy and sorrow
        he was here yesterday
        and she is coming tomorrow

    robert
    pictured in the yearbook — mr. football
    living in the dear departed past
    nancy —
    nancy is prophetic — she's a pisces
    busy with the yarrow stalks she cast
        and the now
        the moment slips away
        gone with its joy and sorrow
        he was here yesterday
        and she is coming tomorrow

    robert
    has a photograph of nancy in his office
    taken on the day that they were wed
    nancy
    goes to see a gypsy fortune teller
    wants to know what's lying up ahead
        and the now
        the moment slips away
        gone with its joy and sorrow
        he was here yesterday
        and she is coming tomorrow

robert
puts away his toothbrush by the mirror
takes a look and sees his hair is gray
nancy
went to sleep in silence — what a pity
they never really lived at all did they?
    they let the now
    the moment slip away
    gone are the joys and sorrow
    but he was here yesterday
    and she
    was
    coming tomorrow

we live together this way

7. THE HYPOTHETICAL QUESTION

lies beside the road like a stone
and probably should be left entirely alone
it being hypothetical
should we bother with what we uncover
while turning it over?

suppose i should ask you
what you think you would do
if all other humans suddenly vanished
leaving you the last of mankind
and with the knowledge that you are the absolute
end of the line
everything else intact though
      supermarkets — libraries
      gas stations — animals
      everything
just as you'd find it today
      minus people

alone
confronting this situation
do you think you'd commit suicide then and there
without hesitation
or do you think you couldn't do that
but most likely you'd wither away
going out of your mind in a very short time
or are you someone who thinks you could
live your life out combing beaches
      a dog at your side — a stick in your hand
      like robinson crusoe
only this time with no hope of finding
      friday's prints in the sand

in short
how much do you think you need your fellow man?
well
      ask a hypothetical question
      get a hypothetical answer

or so i thought
till i was surprised and brought
down in flames
by a braless young girl
a hard line feminist who took aim and said

>boy —
>if i were the one in the problem you posed
>i would not commit suicide
>comb beaches
>nor would i wither away
>those are the options of a male chauvinist
>pig
>
>rather
>i would head for the nearest sperm bank
>and being a healthy female
>impregnate myself
>and start it all over again
>thanks to science this time minus
>men

like i said the hypothetical question
lies beside the road like a stone
and probably should be left entirely alone
but turn it over and usually the usual number
>of salamanders — sowbugs
>>and centipedes will be uncovered
but look out
for an occasional black widow spider
who kills and devours her mate
a fact
that is not in the least bit hypothetical
and in a funny science fiction sort of way
food for thought

>right fellas?

8. FREE AT LAST

if she's part of the movement
she no longer wants to be a girl
      a chick
      or a broad
      not even a lady
she's a feminist
a liberated woman and i'm for this
a free female
means a free male
free enough to openly express
my childish insecurity

      if a person
wants to whine and whimper
now-a-days a person can
but every time i do
my liberated woman says
      act like a man

9. THE TIME SQUEEZE

is a science fiction film
in which john wayne and bette davis
are contemporaries
but the casting director has kept them apart

for john
the leading lady must be freshened like a drink
a testimonial female
a dream inflated with youth
and though he might act differently
she always leaves him exhausted after a love scene
with no one to talk to
except the ghastly remains of ward bond
and gabby hayes

and bette
didn't always cackle that way
forced to play a crazy old crone
once she too had muscle tone and defied gravity
but when a woman's face has been lived in
long enough to have something to say
who would listen
so she makes it up each morning
like a bed
and pays a surgeon to hide the scars

bored with this
the pepsi generation
is out in the lobby buying popcorn
to them it was just another foreign film
they could read the sub-titles
but couldn't understand what they were seeing

and
even i
laughed and cried in all the wrong places
till the houselights came up
and i could see
the back of my own hands

10. WAITING

    i have in my life tried waiting
    in a white room
           for a young working woman
    to bring me color
           through a white door

    it has been a long morning
    with this blank piece of paper
    and quiet guitar
    the sun came crawling on the floor
    and i watched it with no more on my mind
    than you
           and this slow
                      unwinding
                      lonely time

    you will come soon for lunch
    i will hear your sound in the hall
           your hand on the latch
    and then time will fly
           till you're off to work again
           and i am left alone again
    washing the afternoon walls
    with my eyes
    my god
    to be a housewife waiting
           always waiting
                      and you
                      can't create
                      while waiting
                      you can only
                                wait

11. WHITE WATER

    i
who had just entered the rapids
of estrangement
was most interested in what she might say
she
who had just come through the white water
the wild water
the mad crazy part of the river

        now tell me
        for the past few years
        have you encouraged your dear spouse
        to get with it
        and find herself
        and be an entity unto herself?
yes
        and did she do it
        i mean go out and find something of value
        aside from the house
        the children
        and you?
yes
        now tell me
        this strange young unexplainable
        new object of your affection
        is she mostly a pool
        for you to reflect upon?

i would hope there is more to it than that
but
well —
yes
    shit
she said

12. STOP ME IF YOU'VE HEARD IT

a story always looses something
in the second telling
and so
        over the years gladys & j. grabowski
developed a relationship
that needed a third party around
to break the silence
        when the children behaved
        the job secure
        if no one had died
        and the car didn't knock
they lived with the sound of the traffic outside
and the clock

        gladys survived
with the jr. league and a brownie troop
and when the kids grew up she went into group
        j. held on playing golf
till his back wouldn't let him
then feeling his age one day
left home and flew to cleveland on business
checking into a motel
as mr. & mrs. smith
but like the sales pitch says
        after one night in a holiday inn
        you'll not be surprised in the next

in retrospect
i think the grabowski affair
was a suicide attempt on something humdrum
and he going to sleep that night
vaguely wondered
if the maid would arrive in time to turn off the gas
        if she did
        perhaps it would be a good omen
if not —
well a story always looses something
in the second telling.

13. THE BIXBY BRIDGE INCIDENT

the cup was half empty
the big hand said forty-two past
and the word if there was one
was tired
then suddenly the wind touched my hair
and i became aware of myself
there on the bridge
a weary old bird ready to leap
from the nest and fly blind
to the breathing sea
    below
me
in my best bulky-knit sweater
calmly inching forward
a great sadness
in my blue gray eyes
    hair blowing
    aware now
i paused and listened to the night
for motor sound
and looked for lights
but the world was empty
no one was coming to witness
    my final scene
    the grand finale
and it was such a fantastic
dramatic moment
i decided to come back
and tell you all about it

laughing
shaking my head
i drove home
but it wasn't until i saw the shape
of my own house
that i realized the cup
had been half full
    all the time

P.S.

i was told recently
that of all witnessed suicides
from the golden gate bridge
in san francisco, california
not one
not a single person
has been seen to go off on the ocean side
the horizon side
all
as of this writing
have been seen leaping back
toward the city
and that would be a hell of a thing
to discover half way down

once years ago
i hung by my heels
was swatted — whaaaaah — and decided
to suck air and live
on a bridge near big sur, california
in the summer of '71
i faced the same decision again

    and as i write this
    i realize
    i am
    three months old today

14. THE QUALITY OF LOVE

in the throws of the affair
i was surprised to learn
i could love two women
with intensity
at the same time
one with whom i'd spent many years
and one recently met

now
the quality of these loves
is best described by the difference
in my bathroom behavior — toilet procedure
    at home
though the room was occupied
(my wife in the tub)
when ya gotta go
ya gotta go — and i always went
    but in an apartment near chicago
i would carefully close the door
run the water
and turn the fan on

during this time
if a doctor had informed me
i had but six months to live
looking back
i think
i would have chosen
    the apartment
for the first three months
but i know now
i would have wished to go home
to die
    with someone who knows just
    how full of crap
    i really am

15. THE CHICAGO FIRE

No one knows what goes on behind the faces, for I live in your golden shadow blinded by a rush of bright madness, of burning morning haze, and it is a wonder I function at all.

Yet here in virginia I wander down this quiet afternoon with friends and clearly see the dogwood exploding in a galaxy of gray turning green. At my feet tiny flowers, fern and moss are seen in perfect detail.

Far from the midwest we walk at the edge of spring, talking lightly of things voices in the trees, & no one knows that i am being consumed by the thought of you.

      but now
      in another space
          another place and time
      i read the above
          curiously
      like an old newspaper account
      of the chicago fire
      having no idea
      of what it's really all about

      like pain
      such things
      will not be remembered

16. AFTERNOON TV

unable to get going today i allowed myself
time to lie around the house fallow
watching afternoon TV
and my god i had no idea how awful life could be

. . . there was this young lab technician who
wanted to marry a blind girl not because he loved
her which he didn't but because he had fathered
her first child when she'd been married to his
alcoholic brother

. . . the brother in the meantime had developed
lung cancer while in prison but the surgeon who was
to perform the operation was murdered by the blind
girl's mother who had gone mad after being bitten
by a tropical insect that was part of the young lab
technician's experiments

. . . all this happened when the mother tampered
with these experiments hoping to discredit him so
that her daughter might remarry the alcoholic
brother who had quit drinking and what with the
operation and everything needed all the help he
could get . . .

and i sat there dumbfounded
through a soap commercial and the preview
of tomorrow's ON GOING AGONY
after which i got up and went into the bathroom
with a wrench and in two minutes repaired a faucet
that had been leaking for a year and a half
then resting on the edge of the tub admiring
my handiwork i laughed till i cried

> which all goes to prove
> that there ain't no such thing as a happy
> ending but if you're willing to settle for less
> you can have some real good times along the way

17. THE COUNSELOR

i was talking to myself again
in front of the mirror
but the glass man only
moved his lips with mine
and said nothing that would help

so i came to you to hear
what it was i had to tell myself
i chose you above everyone else
because i knew
that you would say

> one can
> only
> help oneself

and that is exactly
the kind of smart-ass remark
i will not take
off a mirror

18. THE TOWER

i had a vision once of a tower
here on the shoulder of this mountain
and i became a wildman with a hammer
                       and a dream
but don't be overly impressed
with men who build towers
there are any number of journeyman
carpenters
              and stonemasons
that can tell you how to do it

the building part is easy
it's the living in it that comes hard

with some simple instruction
anyone can hand a door
but if you know the art
of oiling hinges   teach me

19. A NORMAN KING

middle-aged and bored beyond belief
i went into the brush today
and like a child made myself a clearing

with grub hoe and axe
i fought the undergrowth
and did battle with the greasewood and genista
the going wasn't easy
the bushes striking — slashing back
until the branches brought me crashing down
a whip-like blow across the face

    thanks
    i needed that

then cursing in childish rage
i rise a norman king
to chop and hack
at the very root of my lethargy

take that
    and that
        and that . . . and
slowly — grudgingly
the enemy falls back
until at last i have myself
a piece of open ground

to rest on — to lie upon
and watch the sky from

    listen the wind is cheering

20. WITH A PIERCED EAR

sitting on United — flight 394
with a pierced ear
i find i have velocity and direction

where i have come from i'm not quite sure
where i am going i do not care

the ticket says philadelphia
i'm not there though
i only know i am somewhere
    filled with this feeling
    and aware of it

strange
how i keep leaving behind
the very thing it is that i'm reaching for
    but then life is for living
    time is a spiral
    and every road
    the road home

look for me
i'm coming

finale

. . . And may all dragonflies, codfish and frogs come to this —

BIG SUR
COUNTRY

it is called big sur country
        where i live
and many men of letters have passed through
none have denied its beauty
but few have
        felt at home here

old henry miller — city born
burned his bald head brown
trying to catch the color of the sun
        at partington

like icarus
        he failed and in the end
retired to a cement maze south of here
more at home in an elevator
than at those
        dizzy heights

and jack kerouac
hitched his way along this granite coast

```
          with no real sense of belonging
                    crawling here
                    like an ant
          he found the place a graveyard
          the
             off
                shore
                         rocks
                         tombstones
                         in a ghostly surf
          on the road
          running like a child in the dark
                    hearing things
                    in the bushes
          he hurried north to hide
          in the mulch pits of marin county

          and richard brautigan has come and gone
          and others
                         drawn to and driven off
                         by the size and silence of this place

          but jeffers knew
                    that soaring old predator
                    sharp eyed
          he knew
                    if we could speed
                    time up
                    fast enough
                    we would see
                    that the mountains
                    are dancing
                                and with us
```

LET IT BE A DANCE
(Song poem, music on pages 94, 95)

let it be a dance we do
may i have this dance with you
through the good times
and the bad times too
let it be a dance

let a dancing song be heard
    play the music say the words
        and fill the sky with sailing birds
        and let it be a dance
        learn to follow learn to lead
    feel the rhythm fill the need
to reap the harvest plant the seed
and let it be a dance

    everybody turn and spin
        let your body learn to bend
            and like a willow with the wind
        let it be a dance
a child is born the old must die
a time for joy a time to cry
take it as it passes by
        and let it be a dance

        the morning star comes out at night
            without the dark there can be no light
        and if nothing's wrong then nothing's right
so let it be a dance
let the sun shine let it rain
share the laughter bare the pain
    and round and round we go again
        so let it be a dance

the songs

the price you pay for

Sunflowers

words and music by ric masten

you come out of that place a-gain I gaze in-to your face a-gain try to read your eyes a-gain to-day you walked right in and you sat a while stroked the stri-ped cat a while just as though you'd ne-ver been a-way when i asked you how you'd been you looked up from the cat and then sang a song so ten-der and so strange you closed your eyes and you let it come when you final-ly get it sung you

I offered you a cup of tea
the way that you looked up at me
I knew you hadn't heard a word
I said
your mind so full of crows in flight
and pinwheel spinning starry nights
and no time in the dream to rest your head

but the time is for the ticking clock
and your between the tick and tock
bleeding from the passion in your brain
so put another bandage on
and sing us all another song
and fill us
with the beauty and the pain

of sunflowers
time and time again
I need to spend an hour
with my sunflower friends
sunflowers
light the way
put a touch of color
in the long dark day

the afternoon is dying fast
your songs are bits of flying glass
the colored edges cut into
my eyes
and looking through the salty mist
I saw that you knew how to risk
and father said – all else is a lie

and when you couldn't take no more
you went out through an open door
looking for your blinding field of hay
you left us rich but feeling sad
cause you were sane and we were mad
but i guess
thats the price you pay

for sunflowers

Loneliness

words and music by ric mastin

stan-din' by a high-way waitin' for a ride a bit-ter wind is blow-in' it keeps you cold in-side a line of cars is pas-sin' no one seems to care you look down at your bo-dy to be sure you are there

Chorus: (no chords)

and this is lon-li-ness the kind that i have known if you've had times like this my friend you're not a-lone

sitting in a hotel staring at the walls
with cracks across the ceiling and silence in the halls
you open up the window and turn the TV on
then you go down to the lobby
but everybodys gone

    chorus

so you leave the empty city and go down to the shore
you're aching to discover what you're looking for
the beaches are deserted in the morning time
a solitary figure, you walk the water line

you come upon a tide pool and stand there peering in
and when you touch the water the circles do begin
they lead to where a seabird lies crumpled in the sand
so you take a single pebble and hold it in your hand

    chorus

you come back up the beaches at the end of the day
and see how all your footprints have been washed away
no
nothing is forever
we are born to die
so may i say i love you before i say goodbye

    i must say i love you
    before i say goodbye

Robert and Nancy

words and music by ric masten

Robert buried in the Tribune with his coffee reading all about the day before Nancy just across the table with her teacup she studies what the tea-leaves hold in store

chorus: and the now, the moment slips away — gone with its joy and sorrow he was here yesterday and she is comin' tomorrow we live together this way

robert
pictured in the yearbook - mr football
living in the dear departed past
nancy
nancy is prophetic - she's a pisces
busy with the yarrow stalks she cast

    and the now
    the moment slips away gone with its joy and sorrow
    he was here yesterday and she is coming tomorrow

robert
has a photograph of nancy in his office
taken on the day they were wed
nancy
goes to see the gypsy fortune teller
wants to know whats lying up there ahead

    and the now
    the moment slips away, gone with its joy and sorrow
    he was here yesterday and she is coming tomorrow

robert
puts away his toothbrush by the mirror
takes a look and see that his hair is grey
nancy
went to sleep in silence - what a pity
they never really lived at all did they

    they let the now, the moment slip away
    gone are the joys and sorrow
    but he was here yesterday and she was coming tomorrow

we live together this way

let it be a dance

words and music by ric masten

chorus:

let it be a dance we do may i have this dance with you? through the good times and the bad times too let it be a dance. let a dancing song be heard play the music say the words fill the sky with sailing birds and let it be a dance let it be a dance let it be a dance learn to follow learn to lead feel the rythm fill the need to reap the harvest plant the seed and let it be a dance

everbody turn and spin
    let your body learn to bend
        and like a willow with the wind
    let it be a dance
a child is born the old must die
a time for joy a time to cry
take it as it passes by
    and let it be a dance

    the morning star comes out at night
        without the dark there can be no light
        and if nothing's wrong then nothing's right
so let it be a dance
let the sun shine let it rain
share the laughter bare the pain
    and round and round we go again
    so let it be a dance

        Songs published by
        Mastensville Music
          (BMI)

calligraphy
Rich Hudson

Woodcuts by Ric Masten

BOOKS

Also available on order, through local bookstores that use R. R. Bowker Company BOOKS IN PRINT catalogue system

- ☐ EVEN AS WE SPEAK by Ric Masten. **Paperback $5.50**
  112 pages. ISBN 0-931104-12-2
- ☐ the DESERTED ROOSTER by Ric Masten. **Paperback $5.00**
  96 pages. ISBN 0-931104-11-4
- ☐ STARK NAKED by Ric Masten. ☐ **Paperback $4.95**
  110 pages. ISBN 0-931104-04-1 ☐ **Hardcover $9.95**
- ☐ VOICE OF THE HIVE by Ric Masten. **Paperback $4.95**
  104 pages. ISBN 0-931104-02-5
- ☐ DRAGONFLIES, CODFISH & FROGS **Paperback $5.50**
  Speaking Poems by Ric Masten.
  116 pages. ISBN 0-931104-14-9

RECORD ALBUM

- ☐ Ric Masten Singing **Price $5.50**
  LET IT BE A DANCE
  12 Songs. Stereo SF-1002

BROADSIDES . . . Price .50

Single sheets printed on colored stock. 8½"x11", suitable for framing.

- ☐ The Warty Frog   ☐ Let It Be a Dance
- ☐ The Second Half   ☐ The Homesick Snail
- ☐ Water Spots

PUBLICITY PAMPHLETS

- ☐ Ric Masten in Concert . . . ☐ On the College Campus.
- ☐ In the High School . . . ☐ In the Middle School.
- ☐ In the Elementary . . . ☐ In the Church . . . ☐ On Relationships.
- ☐ Honorarium and Fee Schedule.

CHECKS MADE OUT TO

SUNFLOWER INK
Palo Colorado Canyon
Carmel, CA 93923

ORDER $ _____

6% SALES TAX (CA. RES.) _____

SHIPPING & HANDLING $ ___$1.00___

TOTAL $ _____

Name _____

Address _____

City _____ State _____ Zip _____